D1310166

Stars and Strangers

poems by

Sue Sutherland-Hanson

Finishing Line Press
Georgetown, Kentucky

Stars and Strangers

ACKNOWLEDGMENTS

"Women in the Napa Auto Parts Store" appeared in *Between the Lines*, 2006

"Ahmed, Prince of Peace" was printed in *Chrysanthemum Publications Magazine*, 2009

Versions of "The Gardener" and "Meeting Grandmother Winifred" appeared in *Invitation to Openness*, a self-published book, 2014.

Special thanks to Holly Hughes for midwifing this collection.

Publisher: Leah Maines

Editor: Christen Kincaid

Cover Art: Mariah Hanson Ordonez

Author Photo: Sue Sutherland-Hanson

Cover Design: Elizabeth Maines

Printed in the USA on acid-free paper.
Order online: www.finishinglinepress.com
also available on amazon.com

Author inquiries and mail orders:
Finishing Line Press
P. O. Box 1626
Georgetown, Kentucky 40324
U. S. A.

Table of Contents

For Mom, who gives and receives starlight

A Theology of Seeing: Stars and Strangers...

It is like a pure diamond, blazing
with the invisible light of heaven.
It is in everybody, and if we could see it,
we would see these billions of points of light
coming together. I have no program for this seeing.
It is only given. But the gate of heaven is everywhere.
—Thomas Merton, *Conjectures of a Guilty Bystander*

Perfection dwells in strangers, those we've never met,
the ones who smile or scowl in stores, or stories
on cave walls, tomb-stones, in the font of news,
between the covers of a million books, the stranger
we embrace for a life-time, those that stretch
then leave our wombs, the one that looks back
at you in the mirror through your eyes and those
with leaves, beaks or muzzles, nuzzling or blood-wet.

Though there be darkness, confusion, violence,
nothing wipes clean the prints of that first holder,
or breaks the braid of breath from that first being,
nothing undoes the mystery and truth that we are
of stars, not inert dust but breathing pulses of light,
descending, ascending, smoored to flame,
to that pure point, flickering crystalline and bright
despite darkness or perhaps because of the night.

Our best act of faith is when we expect to see
in another a glimpse, a momentary flash
or to fall prostrate in the brilliance that burns
before us, in our gaze. We can chat with a clerk,
lock eyes with a child, see another's face driving,
nod at walkers, and feel the warmth of torches
lighting stones with running bison or heaven's gates.
Something knows we warm by the hearth of *I Am*.

A Perfect Stranger

> Forget not to show love unto strangers: for thereby
> some have entertained angels unawares.
>   —Hebrews 13:2, *The New Oxford Bible*

We press tight and tired in our tin can car with dust, backpacks,
sweat, quiet and content to be heading home after days absorbing
the earth through boots, tents, trees, and each other. We travel
with a boy, just age thirteen, our charge, and we in our twenties
are fond of him. His head, red and curly, props tired on the pack,
squeezed between us in the back seat. His new man's body, smile,
eager love for life remind us how we want to be forever.

An old Chevy roars onto the road, stopped like a picture.
I see the driver's eyes wide with fear before impact jerks us
hard. Sliding to a high pitched stop, we tumble from our car,
now mangled can, eye each other, panting, shaking... see blood
drip between his brows, a line more red than the boy's hair.

We droop in the pause before ambulance, police flash
and whine arriving. The medics take the boy, leaving
us bleak, lost without our young charge. Our car, shattered
lies like something dead. We stare, silent, unsure until a man
crunches on gravel toward us, tells us he saw the crash,
drove until the voice in his head and his eyes in the mirror
insisted he turn round.

Says he watched himself pull over, spin the wheel in U-turn,
told the police what he saw, now offers a ride to the hospital
where we hear *fractured, six hours of observation*, and see
the boy's sweet head bandaged. We call family, *sorry, so sorry,*
promise to keep them posted. Wait. Wait some more.
Our new friend stays, insists even till two a.m., insists
on driving us to our homes, hours away, to our doors,
mumbles of a chance to do right, won't give a last name.

I cannot remember his first, and cannot remember
the feeling of that night's blood-dark lostness.
His face blurs as if inside the flash of a poor photo.
Was he a being from another realm? The perfection
of the boy and the care of this guardian made me love
the mystery of belonging to this race. What do we need
to know of invisible worlds when there are perfect strangers?

Clamming Friends

We drove in a line of trucks on wet highways,
racing nightfall, then parked on ocean beaches,
whose collusion with the horizon blended
grey sea and sky into *forever*. Sitting on tailgates,
we chatted as we pulled on boots, hopped off
to swing buckets with hundreds, no thousands
of diggers shrunk and managed by immensity.
Silhouettes bent over holes, sorted, searching
for ovals of gold with fat clam necks.

The sky opened, stopped the rain, washed
January's first dusk with pink light. Clouds
lined the moon's procession through the sky,
as it deepened into gold, as hills of razors
climbed to bucket rims. That moon was eager
to join this New Year's night of singing lanterns.

Hugeness filled me—I'll just say it—with *ecstasy*.
Part of me wanted to fall to the sands, Pentecostal,
like the woman I saw as a child, fall, *slain in the spirit*.
She dropped to the floor, dancing horizontal and wild,
trading decorum for joy. My urge to swoon persisted,
but I stayed upright, unwilling to get wet or scare friends.
Besides, I liked smiling in the dark, felt special, saw it
as evidence I was a plain-clothes mystic.

The men cleaned those razors, dipped them,
buttered into flour and fried to perfection.
We straddled benches at the table, holding
platters tall with clams. I watched my friends
glow over candle light, my eyes traveled lines
rivering their cheeks, curving their full-moon bellies.
And then I saw their sacredness, vast as oceans,
abundant with their own secrets, buried in sands
of sea, salt, and spirit, upright and nourishing
as razor clams. I felt a new swoon rising.

Man Over!

we hear midst ferry bells and sirens.
The crew looks deep and brief in each other's eyes,
run fumbling with straps of life-jackets and rafts.
Hearing, *He's over here!* we lean over the rail and see
a diver, staring through his mask beyond us, limp,
buoyant; he slips like water over each wave as hands
and feet wave with the current next to the grebes,
who pay him no mind. *He's dead*, says my husband.

My thoughts scramble to reverse the verdict.
Where's a life ring?! Where's that life boat?!
Why isn't at least one person in the water
to keep this man company, see that he might
yet breathe?! I question if it should be me.

I begin to accept his fate and wonder what he sees,
perhaps himself from above, peaceful and open
to the sky. We watch crew drag him on the raft
then speed him to the shore where EMTs peel his suit,
black rubber to white skin, cover his mouth to give
air his lungs do not receive. I wonder if angels or
dead friends greet him, if he now swims up.

In the seeing, intimacy clings and now connected
to this man's death, I become midwife at his birthing
into the beyond, hold the slippery mystery, this
everyday once-ness of each person's life.

Women in the Napa Auto Parts Store

I'm dark inside my car. Green digits of speed,
yellow ticks of time, and red shapes of warning
should light the dash, but do not, so down aisles
I walk in an auto shop, stacked with boxes,
suspect shapes, male, musty, and foreign.

Two women work the counter, swing 'round to me
like tenders in a quiet bar. They wear tight jeans
and shag haircuts of old rock stars. One cinches
her belt and bulges like a Hubbard squash. The other
hunches. Wide eyes peer through straight straw bangs.

They brighten at my dark tale. Through crooked teeth,
Hubbard says, Y*ou've got a fuse problem, sweetie.*
Energized with purpose, they grab tools, rip open fuses,
and stride out. My car seems happy as one works
under its hood, the other reaches under the dash.

Like a dentist with tweezers and a rotten tooth, Hubbard
holds up a black fuse. They nod, ask me to check the radio.
Nothing, I say. They scowl to ponder. *Wait,* I add,
I forgot to turn the key...it does work. Feeling foolish,
I ask aloud, *What had I been thinking?* They scowl.

Straight-bangs answers, *That's alright honey.* They light
quick smokes and enter to receive their pay. I read
their names on tan shirts, stitched in red cursive,

    Bev. Liz.

I belong to the red that pumps beneath their pockets,
warm as grandmothers who never mocked, sisters who
let girls listen in, daughters who shared their youth.

The till rings open and I pay for the fuse then empty
my purse as an offering, buying gadgets I will never use,
products I don't understand. The point is I leave repaired.

Ahmed, Prince of Peace

Before you boy, I knew so little.
I met a Palestinian once in an airport.
He guessed I was afraid and I was.
Newspapers print black and white
words like *all*, and *terror*, and *revenge*.
I've learned a little since then
of Naomi's poetry,
of Shaheen's music,
of the warmth of chickpea soup,
and the smooth of goat yogurt.

The soldier said he mistook you
for a militant—you—a 12-year-old boy.
Ahmed, he was partly right. When you died,
militant spirits poured out, rampaging
the hospital corridors, demanding
the lurking spirits of death let live
the Arab, the Jew, and the Druse,
who received your lungs, your liver,
your heart.

What did you whisper to your parents
that gave them the courage to love
the children who received these
while you, their own son, lie dying?
What kind of heart beats like yours,
miraculous heart, heart of Christ,
of every true prophet?

When the doctors lifted
the still-pumping heart
from your small body,
true religion fell on its knees,
begging to witness the crown of ages,
lowered on your sweet head.

Ahmed, my prince of peace,
the next Palestinian I meet
will make me think of you,
and I will want to kiss their feet.

Money Teacher

All humans are born entrepreneurs.
—Muhammad Yunus, Nobel Peace Prize Recipient

His wide and laughing smile caught me;
his story kept me. He remains pinned,
black and yellowed news, teaching among
a chaos of favored things layered on cork board,
the rich can *be* and *do* good.

Banker of wealth, baker of hope, candle-stick maker
of Muslim-light in Bangladesh, poster of poverty,
you contradict suspicion of wealth and the moneyed.
I used to pray, Lord, *give me money, enough to be*
free of fear, but not so much that I be enslaved.

Not a bad prayer, but balancing on this beam
lately bruises my feet. What did I care for money
as poet and teacher, nodding at Mary's Magnificat,
God fills the poor and empties the rich? Now, as I decline,
I search for my *Pieta*, a lap to drape my dying form.
Must my children change my diapers, wipe my drool
for lack of wealth to pay a content nurse?

So, I look to you, Yunus, for new prayers, to be
money-wise, to have an easy friendship with wealth,
a friend who comes and goes without embarrassment,
happy to help, wanting to be enjoyed, and I will because
we met through good work, creative joy and gentleness.

Like Balaam, hearing from his mule, might my money
say, *What you want, I cannot give. Stand and feel*
the ground. See what is real. Why wouldn't a friend
speak truth as such? *Yunus*, steward of life lived large,
water me with your wisdom, trickling down. Drops
of peace in words like *Salam daughter, see the vaults,*
joining you to your depth, kin, and infinite, jeweled sky.

A Pakistani Gravedigger

> Don't ask them at all about duty and obligation,
> those for whom God has made love obligatory.
> —Rahman Baba

Taj kneels at his worksite, the *Rahman Baba Graveyard*, named
    for Sufi poet, Pakistani, beloved, and wise. The worker weeps
        on wreaths of chrysanthemums, piled on short mounds of rock.

As a professional rule, Taj never cries at work. He's dug in heat,
    hot as ovens, lowered all ages, height, and weight, but these,
        the children of this school massacre weigh more than any before.

He cannot explain why he weeps, does not know his heart burns
    in compassion, does not know he joins Rahman, who wrote
        to love all, is to *burn like the kabob in the flames of Allah's face.*

Taj works to feed his eight children, but this day, charges no one,
    sees the dead as his own, lines his grief with sweat and asks,
        How could I take money for making the grave of my own child?

Baba, surely you remember Daniel's fiery furnace,
    so assist my prayer. Let Taj, burning for loyalty to love, be held
        and cooled by your angels of perfection, present in his flames.

The Teenage Murderer

> Good and bad are mixed. If you don't have both, you don't
> belong with us.
> —Jelalludin Rumi

I try to avoid news of violence,
don't know why I watched this show.

A convicted teen tells how he
killed a transient under a bridge.

He speaks with boyish candor,
saying he always wanted to be

a doctor, smart and able to help
poor people like his family.

Too young to see the irony
of his crime and dream, too open

to hide his goodness, his innocence,
a small light, pulses on my TV screen.

The moon, circle of light, glows bright
in black expanse that holds dear this pearl,

so as not to overcome. In need
of the other: darkness and light.

Translators

We were set on opposite sides of a political fence—
my native friends, fishing on Judge Boldt's side,
my father, a gillnetter, on the other, branded racist,
for testifying against that decision. Of course
I didn't bring that up when I met K, office whiz,
princess from the Kwikilsutainuk Tribe, born
to a chief, who commanded she learn only English.

He didn't know her destiny as translator.

Siblings, cousins, uncles and aunts held K
as they sang tribal lullabies and whispered
the language of their heart into hers. She grew
in her art, translating life like an alchemist.
To those who would listen, she stopped taunts
of children deriding her friends, their fish smell,
opened eyes to native healing, expanded the air
with her stories of ghosts, elders drumming, dancing

to her songs at a totem dedication at the Old Paramount.

She translated addiction, abuse, and grief into strength,
straight-backed, gentle, merry, and motherly. She heard
my muted despair as a mother, lost in a family storm,
she walked 'round her desk, grasped my shoulders, told
what I must do to survive and lead my family home.
My back grew strong at her touch and like Pentecost,

I understood her fierce dialect of love. It saved us all.

Now at the bus stop, I stand with a native Grandmother,
perhaps S'Klallam. We speak of football, the weather,
her husband, diabetic and failing. We laugh as the children
race round us for tag. Her son drives by, reckless, smiles
with bad teeth, a sullen women next to him. Grandmother
shakes her head, worried, then holds her grandson's gaze
as he asks if he should be a quarterback for the Seahawks.

He hears endurance in their talk of football.

I find myself praying her strength enters the air,
for my lungs to inhale and exhale in my home.
Don't we all suffer the yellow teeth of addiction
and bruises from lies that we are not enough?
The straight back of this bus-stop grandmother,
her laugh, and words of nurture remind me of K.
They translate poverty into potlatch, burn fences
between us, and offer gifts I understand through

grandmothers' art of translation.

The Widower from Choir

> You don't feel like your best self when you fall apart,
> but you have to fall apart to become your best self.
> — Richie Norton

We sang with him, jaunty retiree, in the church choir,
a chemist of metals, a confident man, who oft spoke
of years in the college glee club. He played tennis,
spry, in control, exuded wavy-haired charm bordering
on arrogance. He leapt at solos, corrected mates freely
while his wife, J. smiled, proud of her prince charming.

I saw him the other day, years later, frail,
standing vacant by his car in the market lot.
I didn't wave. Last time I saw him with J.,
he'd forgotten who I was. Or was it her?
One of them tried to explain our connection.
We parted embarrassed. I met him cart to cart

in bulk foods by the nuts where he looked at me
hard. I'd heard his wife passed, prompted him
to remember me, saying I'd sung with him years ago,
said I was sorry 'bout J's passing, how it must be hard.
He shook his head, mumbled thanks, how he's better.
At least now I can say her name without... he stopped,
ran fingers down his cheeks in the path of tears.

Moved, I mumbled, *life can be hard. Yes*, he agreed,
*this is the hardest thing. I've been back to choir three times
and do you know, I couldn't make heads or tails of the music.
The second time, I got the words but not the notes,
and the last time, I could sing again.*

I asked how old he was and he opened his mouth,
but no words came out. Defeat clouded his face
as he struggled to remember. Finally he gave up,
it's a terrible thing not to remember your own age.
I joked we could all use fresh minds like my grandson's,
as I touched the four-year-old, sitting in the cart.
The man smiled sadly, *I need a new brain.*
As we rolled our separate ways, he added, *Oh,*
I still do technical writing. That's been good.

Less concerned after hearing that, I still needed
to check my list to stay on task. His story 'round loss
and losing replaced *spaghetti, half-and half,* and *carrots.*
We passed again in front of the pasta, and without pause
he said, *I'm 86.* I turned, watched him walk jaunty steps.
I cupped my grandson's chin and set my list down.

Of a Feather

> I saw the spirit descend like a dove from the sky
> and it came to rest on him.
> —John 1:32, *The New Oxford Bible*

A Canada goose lifts from a field,
pumps her wings, fans with rushing air
commuters stuck in traffic. We look up,
cooled, and for a moment,
lifted.

A great blue heron tilts his head,
slow-motion fishes my pond.
I have never done anything
with that much
patience.

The sweet-faced mallard leads
her shrinking line of ducklings, babes
lost to raccoons, drainage grills, snakes.
She never stops her throaty call, giving
comfort.

The lark piccolos a showy twill;
a jazz musician in his throat
sends notes to dance under my heels,
make my feet light. My ears can't stop
laughing.

The forest pigeon in creamy voice
calls *hooo-hoo.* After a full day,
caring hard from dawn to dusk,
my heart hears *shhhhhhhhh,*
rest.

A red hawk stretches low over the trail,
shows talons and down belly. What if
clutched in death, my cheeks feel
this softness, then of my end, I'd have
no fear.

The Cyclist

Autumn brings groups of cyclists flowing
like schools of tropical fish bright
in air blue as the Caribbean.

Thighs thick as trees squeeze in tight shorts,
whiz quiet on high-tech bikes flowing
under bent backs; racers blur down my rural road.

I must enter the flow of these speedsters,
so I bide my time in the car, watch
for space, for my chance to *share the road*,

but the sighting of a hermit neighbor stops me.
Hunched over fenders rusty and round,
he pedals fat tires awkward with low tech effort.

One leg of his overalls scrunches up to his knee,
dark hairs stubble his shin rising thin from his boot.
His beard wraps round his neck blending

like snakes into unkempt hair dancing
to the flapping garbage-bag snapping wild
from his bike basket. I laugh at the surprise,

the second-looks, and wobbled paths as riders
in muscled uniforms catch the shock of him,
one shoulder strap unhooked, slaps free.

He churns through the group, pays no-one any mind,
turns cross current onto his lane as his broad back
dips and bumps over pot holes. This rock cod

flowing foreign and brown in a neon stream intrigues,
and yes, his madness elsewhere could frighten,
but here on my road, his indifference inspires.

For the Person Cooking at the Edge of the Woods

Rare morning of marvel, I pump whole-grain legs
grateful and strong jogging organic trails

floating in piney air my lungs inhale deep
hungry after a night of making light and love

in dreams where the lanterns of Hafiz hung.
The salal catches wind of it all—waves green

in my passing breeze. The puddles recede
their fine black mud to a reasonable depth

where my dog stands to raise her nose and smiles
to smell wisps of scent from someone cooking.

I too smell this smoke of frying welcome, picture
biscuits and gravy. Aromas from this fare waft

and twirl images of morning spreads to celebrate
this day. I change course from counting calories

and steps, turn to join the woodsman's brunch by
jogging back to the car to drive to the market café.

The dog curls on her blanket where she dreams
of biscuits and gravy that I order to honor her,

and the gift, good as frankincense and myrrh
carried by wise men, this sausage scent of lure.

Keeping Vigil

She sits silent, back bent against her season of dying,
unrelenting, leans against her hardest winter yet,
weakens in the wear of each day, shuffles expectant
'round time's bend, surprised not to find death yet.

It's hard to see her wait—hard this letting go, more
letting go. But, were she stronger and we found her
gone, wouldn't we wail, *it's too soon for dying; she was
so alive?* This way we pace life's fence-line with her,

wonder about our own deaths. Will we weaken
while loved ones worry, perish in smashing cars
or gulp freezing seas replacing air? Will we drop
mid-sentence or crawl wheezing into the beyond?

Even though we watch her stare into the clear expanse,
we'll gasp, shocked she found the opening and left.

The Gardener

He hoes, plants, cuts, prunes, piles,
hauls, and digs for work and at home
for he loves the garden—its zebra grass,
geraniums, lilac, hydrangea, fuchsias,
cedars, fig, camellias, dogwood, fir
and wild cranberry.

For my part, I love the earth and air
that sweeps in with him, his shoulders
and back covered in tree dust and mulch.
I admire the patterns he mows in the lawn,
the elegant gate to yellows, reds, blues,
pinks and purples that glory in their keep
and color, but this is not enough for him;

he wants me to feel the hard, soft soil,
wonder at the seed, wait for the wisp
of sprout, pride in the height of the bean
stalking round the pole, curl the tendrils
of my attention on the peas *I* planted.
To this end, he builds raised beds of timber,
piles them full with hens' manure, hoes it fine
and asks me to plant the summer garden.

I accept, find myself marveling at speckles
of seeds, muse as I poke peas and corn into
the ground, pour carrot flecks into soft soil rows.
I know I take credit for many things,
mostly given, and smile when I hear him
call the vegetable garden *mine.*

Meeting Grandmother Winifred

My sister told me she felt the presence
of Grandmother Winifred, grieved
by her short life, dying at age thirty-six,

unable to deliver her eighth child alive,
sad that her children grew motherless.
I shivered at the story of this apparition.

Why, I wondered, wasn't grandma in
a cloud of witnesses, seeing the rightness
of life beyond the living? I summoned

our crying ghost to whisper reprimands.
Grandma, why don't you see beyond
the living? It's not right you grieve fate.

Wouldn't it be better to send us means
to break the hardpan-lie that says our lives
do not matter? Grandma, you know

I suffer seasons when I hate my finiteness,
mediocrity, inability to stop the wounding
I cause and receive in binding pattern.

You know how I plug my ears against that ticking,
announcing, as I imagine, a shrill bell ringing:
times up, life's over! Today I cried my prayers

because of you. I need you to stop, sad ghost,
your head-hanging, your moaning that life
was not enough. How hard to believe we matter.

Grandma, my prayer of tears calmed my fears
about the after-life. In silence, I was invited
to enter the sky through holes of passing clouds

to stand with you. We watched our patch grow
vast and clear in blue reality, dissolving the mirage
of insufficiency, unlocking prisons of how we think

life should go. To a cliff we traveled, banked
on the Straits of Juan de Fuca, where winds
pushed and blazed us forward. You stood

next to me with your children, theirs, and mine,
chins up, breathing dignity, knowing life is
enough. We watched you join the witnesses

in that cloud, celebrating your short life,
lived well enough. You left and we knew
you would then stop visiting us with tears.

The Hag

> I think we are well advised to keep on nodding terms
> with the people we used to be, whether we find them
> attractive company or not.
>
> Joan Didion, *Slouching Towards Jerusalem*

She came when the moon
pulled my cycles, launched

her assaults, clutched my elbow,
crowded my step, squeezed

beside me in the pew, wheezed
all manner of complaints.

She served communion
too close to me, criticizing all.

She questioned my giving
a ferry ticket as help

for the poor, traveling
to an interview or clinic.

Yes, help them leave.
Embarrassed, I scraped

at her, like barnacles,
sucked to my back,

but this only wounded.
Wisdom reasoned, *if you*

love her, you can love
anyone, but I could not.

In time, I learned
it was enough simply

to stand near her, let the divine
reach wide and embrace us both.

Poet Care

She likes to ooze gentle poems with soft sounds,
smiling, beaming white piled puffs of clouds,
comfort, on which to light, float, lay our face.

Yet, the grit in her craw hopes she's real enough
to fork tough bites, stick the ones that chuck, buck,
fuck, tick and tock—in those crocodiles that dog
the living with snapping jaws and swallowed clocks
with springs rusting, winding down, ...*kaput.*

Grief is hard to swallow, needing consonants
that scrape sounds to scratch ears, give teeth
to chew the gristle well. She is better at gentle,
likes wrapping soft poems 'round sore hearts,
but when life bites hard, she wants to twist
'round and clamp with a muscled bite back,
be the she-bear circling cubs with fur and
claws, write as a poet with a strong jaw.

Prodigal Body

> ...while he was still a long way off, his father saw him
> and felt compassion, and ran to embrace and kiss him.
> Luke 15:20, *The New Oxford Bible*

My body didn't come home like the prodigal son for fare
better than slop, and I didn't party with rings of welcome.

It was more subtle, like a private truce, much needed
and a long time coming. Near sixty, there's a new ease

in our life together. When I was young and deaf
to the gift of my body, it disappeared best it could,

rising irrepressible as blood moon of cramps,
headaches, soreness, embarrassing attractions

from loneliness or loyalties beyond my knowing.
More and more, I shake my head at the miracle

of my children. What else can I call my body
creating two entire humans without my mind?

I don't know exactly when I turned to listen or why,
but what it knows, how it speaks on all subjects,

amazes: healing, marriage, friendship, and joy.
My body always wanted to be near my beloved's,

but I made it complicated until, coming to my senses,
I saw to miss this warmth denied life, a loss for fools.

Maybe all repentance, deciding it is time to turn, face
a new direction, comes from seeing our impending end.

A sad clarity began when I saw life would soon part us.
Regretting lost time, I now bow to the creaturely me.

I am the one returning, skin robes set upon my shoulders.
We will return to dust, but my bones know, to form a star.

End Notes:

"Clamming Friends:" The Pentecostal movement in the United States founded churches with an emphasis on the presence of the Holy Spirit evidenced by speaking in tongues, dancing in the spirit, or falling in a swoon, known as 'slain in the spirit'.

"Ahmed, Prince of Peace:" The AP story entitled, *"Palestinian Boy's Organs Donated to Israeli Patients,"* was in *The Kitsap Sun* on November 8, 2005. In 2011, Heart of Jenin, a documentary film of this event was made.

"The Money Teacher:" Muhammad Yunus won the Nobel Peace Prize in 2006 for his work as an economist. He wrote, *Banker to the Poor* and *Creating a World without Poverty*.

Balaam, a Syrian prophet in the *Book of Numbers* in the Hebrew Scriptures advises the Moabites to let the Israelites alone since they are blessed. During a trip where Balaam travels to confer with the Moabites, his donkey refuses to proceed despite his beatings. The animal has stopped for it sees an angel standing before it and turns and speaks to Balaam about the vision. This opens Balaam's eyes to the presence of the angel.

"The Pieta" is a subject in Christian art depicting the Virgin Mary cradling the dead body of Jesus.

"The Gravedigger:" Judaism, Christianity, and Islam , the monotheistic faith traditions share many of the same sacred stories and prophets like the story in *Daniel* of Shadrach, Meshack, and Abednego, who were thrown in a fiery furnace. The story goes, they did not perish; they were seen walking in the flames in the company of angels.

"Translators:" Judge Boldt interpreted the Medicine Creek Treaty to favor Northwest native fishing rights over non-native fishermen, whose protests in response were called the Fish Wars in the 1970's.

-*Pentecost* refers to a Biblical story in the *Book of Acts* which tells of the Holy Spirit entering a room of diverse Jews with the sound of rushing wind. The Spirit appeared as flames of fire above each person, allowing them to understand each other despite their different languages.

"Meeting Grandmother Winifred:" Saint Paul used the term *Cloud of witnesses* in his letter to the *Hebrews* in chapter 12: 1-2. He was referring to the presence of ancient prophets and ancestors who are alive and supportive from the beyond the lives of humans searching for what is true and real.

Sue Sutherland-Hanson grew up in a fishing family in Port Townsend, a small town shored by the Puget Sound and the Straits of Juan de Fuca. She holds a Bachelor of Arts in French Literature, a Master of Arts in Teaching English to Students of other Languages (ESL) and a Masters of Divinity. In seminary, Sue focused on the sacred texts, theology, stories, practices, and the arts that explore questions about the mystical in life and how we relate to ourselves, each other, the ancients, the earth, the universe, and the Divine.

Sue was a regular blogger for *Spirited Women* and co-authored her first collection of poems, *Invitation to Openness—Poems for Individuals and Communities Seeking the Sacred in the Present Moment*. Her poems have been published in *Between the Lines, Chrysanthemum Press, Poetry Corners, Ars Poetica,* and *Floating Bridge Press*.

In addition to writing, Sue teaches workshops on writing as a listening practice, sacred creativity, the wisdom of the body, labyrinths, and Celtic spirituality. When not writing or teaching, she enjoys walking, leading groups on pilgrimage, officiating weddings, or playing with her grand-children.

CPSIA information can be obtained
at www.ICGtesting.com
Printed in the USA
BVHW03s1804200618
519552BV00001B/65/P

9 781635 340327